Contents

Preface

Considering the fact that our history has not always been the happiest, it might seem peculiar to an outsider that there have been so many songs of a comical nature written and popular in Ireland; but then we might admit to be a peculiar people who laugh and make jokes in adversity, and cry in happier times. At any rate the comic song has remained abidingly popular at festive gatherings, supplemented by songs which, while not directly comical in theme, have the benefit of a rousing chorus in which everyone can join. Both types make up the songs in this book.

I have done my best to give credit where credit is due and, where at all possible, discover the authors of these effusions: it is not always possible as sometimes the origins are quite obscure, or go back a long while. If any acknowledgements have inadvertently been omitted I hope this note will be taken as an apology.

James N. Healy
December 1985

1. Biddy MacGrath's Bra

Words: Taken down from the singing of Flor Dullea
Music: 'Mrs MacGrath

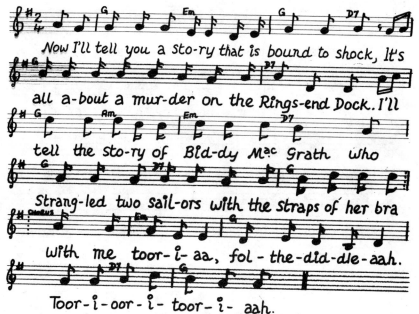

Now I'll tell you a sto-ry that is bound to shock, It's
all a-bout a mur-der on the Rings-end Dock. I'll
tell the sto-ry of Bid-dy Mac Grath who
Strang-led two sail-ors with the straps of her bra
with me toor-i-aa, fol-the-did-dle-aah.

Toor-i-oor-i-toor-i-aah.

They tried to dope her with foreign liquor
But even at that they couldn't lick her
She remembered she was told by her Ma and Da
To keep both of her hands on the straps of her bra.

She put the straps of her bra around the big fellas neck
And tossed him in the Liffey like a crust of bread
Then the small fella came up and said 'Hee-Haw'
So she stuffed his gob with the rest of her bra.

She went home that night about a quarter to one
Happy and contented with a job well done
She told the story to her Ma and her Da
They said: 'Thank God that you wore your bra.'

Now come all you young girls who like a sailor by night
Never wear the straps of your bra too tight
Remember the story of Biddy MacGrath
– Keep both of your hands on the straps of your bra.

I got this from the occasionally untuneful but highly amusing singing of my friend Flor Dullea at Group Theatre private sessions. Flor doesn't recall where he got it from; but it is reminiscent of slightly bawdy student days, and to the same tune as the well-known 'Mrs MacGrath'.

2. The Glendalough Saint

Words and Music: Traditional

But as he was fishin' one day
A catchin' some kind of a trout, sir,
Young Kathleen was walking that way,
Just to see what the saint was about, sir.
'You're a mighty fine fisher,' says Kate
'Tis yourself is the boy that can hook them
But when you have caught them so nate,
Don't you want some young woman to cook them?'
Right foldidle doldidle dol, etc.

'Be gone out of that,' said the saint,
'For I am a man of great piety,
Me character I wouldn't taint
By keeping such class of society.'
But Kathleen wasn't goin' to give in
For when he got home to his rockery
He found her sittin' there in,
A-polishing up of his crockery
Right foldidle doldidle dol, etc.

He gave the poor creature a shake,
Oh! I wish that the peelers had caught him;
He threw her right into the lake,
And of course she sank down to the bottom.
It is rumoured from that very day,
Kathleen's ghost can be seen on the river;
And the saint never raised up his hand,
For he died of the right kind of fever.
Right foldidle doldidle dol, etc.

I remember my sister singing this (suitably out of tune, if she will forgive me for saying so) when she and I were children.
Apparently the old saints had a lot more fun than we give them credit for!

3. The Finding of Moses

Words and Music: Adaptation of original by M. Moran (Zozimus)

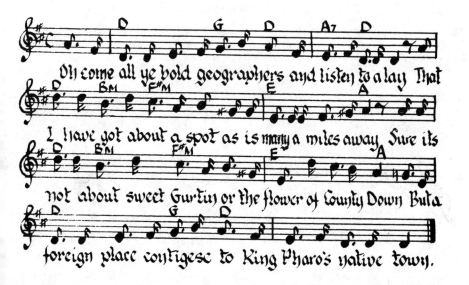

Oh come all ye bold geographers and listen to a lay That
I have got about a spot as is many a miles away Sure its
not about sweet Gurtin or the flower of County Down But a
foreign place contigese to King Pharo's native town.

At a spot in Egypt's land that's right convenient to the Nile,
Old Pharaoh's daughter with her maids went out to bathe in style,
'Oh! come now strip off my duds,' says she, and that was speedy done
It was gettin' them stuck on again that used to start the fun.

When her wrappin's were removed and she prepared to face her bathe
She made a playful leap and gave her lovely hands a wave,
But her foot caught on a cactus sprig growin' from the virgin sod,
And the yell she gave would from the grave raise up the sons of Nod.

Well, when she found her depth she turned her back unto the land
And for to dry her royal pelt she ran along the sand.
Till stumbling by a bulrush clump and lookin' down she found
There a starin' smilin' baby in a basket on the ground.

She was desperate fond of childer as was more than plain to see,
For she cried, 'Sweet babe, this Nile you'll have, and come along with me,'
As a child and mild and always wild her wish did not deny,
And tho' young in speech within its reach it had a powerful cry.

Oh! all back then in the palace Pharaoh said, 'What's this, me child?'
'Sure I call him Moses, sir,' she said, 'for I took him from the Nile.'
Poor old Pharaoh got discoloured and the maids stood in a hush,
'Ah! that's news to me,' says Pahraoh, 'what about the gooseberry bush.'

'Whose child is this?' she cried and raised her royal eyes aloft,
But the maids just sniffed and winked their eyes and said you're queer and
        soft;
And they made no more palaver till she screeched out queer and wild,
'Ah! Now tearin' ages tell me now which one of yiz owns the child.'

The most famous song of a real-life character, 'Zozimus' (Michael Moran), the blind and eccentric
Dublin street ballad maker (c. 1794-1846). This version, with emphasis on the comic, is from the late
Sean F. Healy's collection, which he left to me some twenty-five years ago.

10

4. The Tinker's Budget

Words and Music: Traditional

Come all you good people and I will relate A comical story that happened of late, It's not very short or it's not very long But perhaps it may come to a verse of a song with a fal de del dor rel lee dor rel i dee.

It happened one day down in the main street
When a whole band of tinkers they chanced for to meet;
There was tinkers from Kerry and tinkers from Clare,
From Cork and Tipperary and the divil knows where. *Chorus*

When those tinkers they met they began for to chat –
English and Irish and the divil knows what:
Like birds of one feather they all did agree,
To go down to Tom Daltons for a bit of a spree. *Chorus*

When those tinkers went in to the crowd in the hall
For the best of the whisky those tinkers did call;
They drank and they spent 'till their money was gone,
And one of the tinkers he thought of a plan. *Chorus*

Saying: 'My jolly comrades, shure I must depart,
And when I return I'll fill you a quart.'
He shouldered his budget and never cried stop
'Till he knocked at the door of a pawnbroker's shop. *Chorus*

Saying: 'Now, Mr Murphy, I've met with a friend
Who says you're in habit of money to lend,
So lay by my budget, my hammer and shears,
And give me the price of a gallon of beer.' *Chorus*

The tinker's ould budget lay close to the wall
In a few minutes after the babe gave a bawl;
The pawnbroker started and said to his wife,
'There's a child in the budget I'll wager my life.' *Chorus*

11

The town it was searched and the tinker was found,
The pawnbroker said then: 'Well I'll give him five pounds
To take back his budget his hammer and shears,
And allow for the price of one gallon of beer.'   *Chorus*

The pawnbroker from laughing he could not forbear.
He presented the baby before the Lord Mayor.
The Lord Mayor from laughing he nearly fell dead,
Thinking how the ould budget it was brought to bed.   *Chorus*

Collected from Paddy O'Shea who heard it from John Burns (1852-1947) near Tahilla. Burns may have brought it from Limerick about ninety years ago. A tinkers 'budget' is the bundle he used carry on his back. Burns was known as 'Garryowen' because when he came back from Limerick he used to sing the song of that name.

5. The Twangman

Words and Music: Traditional, Dublin

Oh, come lis-ten to- me sto-ry, 'tis a-bout a nice young man when the Mel-ee-sha was-n't watch-in' he dealt in hawking twang He lov'd a love-ly maid-en as fair as any midge; An' she Kep' a Treac-le Billy depot wan side a' the Car-lisle Bridge

Another wan came coortin' her,
His name was Mickey Bags,
He was a commercial traveller,
An' he dealt in bones and rags.
He took her out to Sandymount
To see the waters rowl,
An' he stole the heart of the twangman's girl
Playin' Billy-in-the-Bowl!

Now when the twangman heard of that
He flew into a terrible rage,
An' he swore by the contents of his twang cart
That on him he'd have revenge.
So he lay in wait near James' gate,
An' when poor Bags came up,
With his twang knife he tuk the lief
Of the poor ould gather'em-up!

A typical Dublin type street ballad to the tune of The Cruise of the Calabar.
It dates from around the middle of the last century, and the words come from an old ballad sheet.

13

6. Paddy Doyle's Ass

Words and Music: Old Ballad Sheet

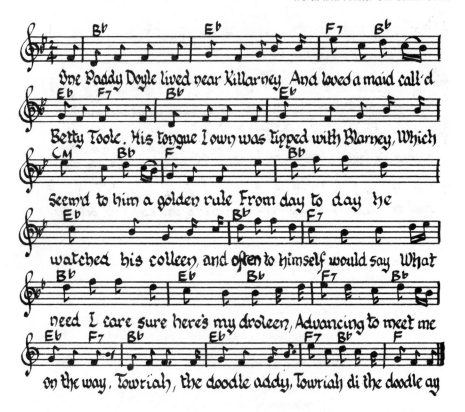

One Paddy Doyle lived near Killarney, And loved a maid call'd Betty Toole. His tongue I own was tipped with Blarney, Which Seem'd to him a golden rule. From day to day he watched his colleen, and often to himself would say. What need I care sure here's my droleen, Advancing to meet me on the way. Towriah, the doodle addy, Towriah di the doodle ay

One heavenly night in last November,
   The moon shone gently from above,
What night it was I don't remember,
   But Paddy went to meet his love.
That day Paddy took some liquor,
   Which made his spirits light and gay,
Says he, 'What use my walking quicker?
   Sure I know she'll meet on the way.'

So he turned his pipes and fell a-humming,
   As slowly onwards he did creep,
But fatigue and whiskey overcame him,
   So down he lay and fell asleep.
But he wasn't long without a comrade
   And one that gave him out the pay,
For a big jackass smelled out poor Pat,
   And lay down beside him on the way.

14

He stretched his arms out on the grass,
  A-thinking on his little dear,
He dreamt of comforts without number
  Coming on the ensuing year.
He stretched his arms out on the grass,
  His spirits felt so light and gay,
But instead of Bet, he gripped the ass,
  And he roared: 'I have her any way.'

He hugged and smugged his hairy messer,
  And flung his old hat at woe and care,
Says Pat, 'She's mine, the heavens bless her,
  But pon my soul, she's mighty quare,
But I think,' said Pat, 'it's time to rise,'
  With that the ass began to bray.
Pat jumped up and opened his eyes.
  Saying: 'Who served me in such a way?'

Like blazes then away he cut
  At railway speed or as fast I'm sure,
But he never stopped a leg or foot
  Until he came to Betty's door.
By this time now 'twas dawning morning,
  So down on his knees he fell to pray,
Saying, 'Let me in, och, Betty darling,
  For I'm kilt – I'm murdered on the way.'

So he up and told her all quite civil,
  While she prepared a brimming glass,
About how he hugged and smugged the devil
  Says she, 'Sure that was Doran's ass.'
And, 'So I believe it was,' says Pat,
  So they got wed on the very next day,
But she never got the new straw hat
  That the jackass ate upon the way.

A typical mid nineteenth century narrative ballad which I got from an old song sheet. The tune is an amalgam of several popular songs of its period. It is about a donkey, not about a part of Pat's anatomy.

15

7. When Pat came over the Hill

Words and Music: Samuel Lover

Oh! when Pat came ov-er the hill, his Col-een fair to see, His whis-tle low but shrill the sig-nal was to be — 'Oh, Ma-ry' her moth-er cried,—'there is some-one whist-lin' sure,' 'oh, moth-er it is the wind you know that's whis-il-ing thro' the door'— with me fol-did-dle-lad-dle-ay; me fol-did-dle-lad-dle-ah, me fol-did-dle-lad-dle ay, hey fol-did-dle, lol-da-la-lee ———.

'I've lived a long time, Mary, in this wide world, my dear,
But the door to whistle like that I never yet did hear';
'But, mother, you know the fiddle hangs close beside the chink,
And the wind upon the strings is playing a tune, I think.'
   Chorus:

'The dog is barking now; the fiddle can't play the tune.'
'But mother, you know they say dogs bark whenever they see the moon':
'But how can he see the moon when he is old and blind,
Blind dogs don't bark at the moon, my dear, nor fiddles don't play with the wind.'
   Chorus:

'And now I hear the pig, uneasy in his mind.'
'But mother, you know they say that pigs can see the wind';
'That's all very true, my dear, but I think you may remark,
That pigs no more than we can see anything in the dark.'
   Chorus:

16

'I'm not such a fool as you think; I know very well 'tis Pat;
Go home you whistlin' thief and do get away out o' that;
And you go into bed, don't plague me with your jeers;
For although I've lost my sight, I haven't lost my ears!'
   Chorus:

And you lads when courting going, for your sweetheart's sake,
Take care not to whistle too loud in case the old woman might wake;
For the days when I was young, forget it I never can,
I knew the difference between a fiddle, a dog and a man.
   Chorus:

Samuel Lover (d. 1868) was one of the first 'one-man' performers, singing his own songs and telling his own stories. Nowadays people are inclined to dismiss him as being 'stage-Irish' but that I suppose was the fashion of his time and many of his songs (for instance The Low Back'd Car *which is* **in** Ballads from the Pubs of Ireland) *are catching and attractive.*
   In theme this one is not unlike The Spinning Wheel.

8. The Codfish

Words and Music: Traditional

Now there was an old la-dy liv-in' on the hill; if She is-nt dead she's liv-in' there still, with me Tow-row-de-ra-ddy o Tow-Row-de-rad-dy o, Tow-row-de-rad-dy Oh, Der-ee —

She spied three fishermen fishing one day
Now she didn't say a word, but she let them fish away. *Chorus:*

Fishermen, fishermen, fishermen three
You wouldn't have a codfish that you would let to me? *Chorus:*

She caught the ould codfish by the backbone
She threw him o'er her shoulder and scraddled off home *Chorus:*

She had no place to put him in saucer or a griddle
So she put him in the place where Johnny used to piddle. *Chorus:*

When Johnny got up to make what he had
Up stood the codfish and he grabbed him by the lad. *Chorus:*

Oh! Mary, oh Mary, you divil hurry hether
For the codfish in the skellet have me caught by the leather! *Chorus:*

So Mary got the ladle, and Johnny got the stick
But the more they hit the codfish the more he held his grip! *Chorus:*

So now to conclude and finish my joke
They had beaten the codfish till they had the chamber broke. *Chorus:*

Collected at a riotous ballad session at Lyracroumhane, in the depth of the Kerry hills from **Con** O'Sullivan.
Not perhaps reserved for the most polite society! So don't let your mother hear you.

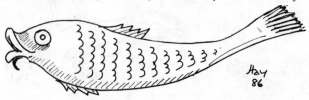

18

9. The Chinaman

Words and Music: Collected by Colm Ó Lochlainn

By what the lawyer says to me, me gold would fill a coach,
And I've eighteen wives already, awaitin' me approach.
What they are like I cannot tell, but one thing I will own.
If he'd willed them all to someone else, more friendship he'd have shown.

I'm going to have me eyebrows shaved one hour befoe I sail,
And I'll wear me hair in one long plait, like Rooney's donkey's tail.
I think I'll make a nice Chinee when I have learned their way,
Providin' they don't hurt me with their strong gunpowder tay.

And should you care to drop a line, in memory this retain,
Address to 'Ling Chung Chang Awong' that's me Chinese maiden name
I'll found an Irish colony, in this outlandish part
So *Beannacht leat*; goodbye to all, it's time for me to start.

Collected by Colm Ó Lochlainn this most unusual but amusing ballad was obtained by him from his printing foreman, John Keegan.

One doesn't often hear of an Irishman adventuring to China, but I doubt if young Mr Clancy would have found things as he imagined they might be!

10. The Tipperary Tinker

Words: As sung by Denis McCarthy
Music: 'The Galbally Farmer'

I'm a wan-der-ing tin-ker I've trav-elled me share   and I

Cour-ted the lassies from Ant-rim to Clare   I was

always light-heart-ed and I had'nt a care   and I

Sang with the birds in the morn-ing; Till Cupid came sport-ing one

morning in May - I spied a fair las-sie as   I

went on my way and the mom-ent I saw her my

heart went a-stray and Comm-enc'd for to thump without

warn-ing. Skiddl-ee-i-do, and skiddle-ee-i-do dar-um H'm

Skid-dle-ee-I-do-and Skid-dle-ee-um-du-dah-du-doh-dam, and
Skiddle-ee-um-de, Skid-dle um-doh dar-um

I drew up beside her and blushing with shame
I gently enquired if she'd tell me her name.
'Oh, begad, now,' said she, 'I will tell you the same
All the people I know call me Mary.
But me father has got me a man in his eye
Who has acres of land, and a fortune for I:
And he says that for me he'd be willing to die –
And his name is Alphonsus O'Leary.'

'I know him,' say I, 'he has land; he has gold,
But look at the creature, sure he's withered and old,
And an old man's affections are always quite cold
Although he'd be wed to a fairy;
But look at meself, sure I'm handsome and tall,
And I know that you'd love me the best of 'em all,
So come, don't be hidin' your head in your shawl
And say that you'll marry me, Mary.'

Oh she blushed, and she giggled and said, 'You're a rogue,'
And her sweet lilting laughter was soft as her brogue,
She said, 'I'd exchange all his gold for one pogue
From the tinker from sweet Tipperary.'
So together we went to the priest to be wed,
And between us a cross word has never been said:
While the rich count their gold we count childer instead,
And we pray for Alphonsus O'Leary.

Oh come all ye maidens and listen to me –
Let the man that you marry be youthful and free,
'Tho he'd have as much gold as there's fish in the sea
Sure an old man is always contrary.
He'll say that he's right, and that you must be wrong,
And 'tis worse that he'll get as the years roll along;
So if you want to make all of your life a sweet song
Go and marry a tinker like Mary.

This ballad received lively treatment from Denis MacCarthy, who had tremendous rhythm to his voice, at ballad sessions at the Group Theatre. I have never heard it sung by anyone else, and as far as I am aware this is its first time in print. The tune resembles The Galbally Farmer *but is not quite the same.*

11. The Foggy, Foggy Dew

Words: This version James N. Healy
Music: Traditional

Now I am a ba-che-lor I live all a-lone and I
work at the weav-er's trade, and the
on-ly on-ly thing that I e-ver did wrong was to
woo a fair young maid I woo'ed her in the
Sum-mer time, and most of the win-ter too— and the
on-ly, on-ly thing that I ev-er did wrong was to
save her from the fog-gy, fog-gy dew.

One night she crept into my bed
When I lay fast asleep
She threw her arms around my neck
And then began to weep
She sighed, she cried, she damn near died
And what was I to do?
But to hold her in my arms the whole night through
Just to save her from the foggy, foggy dew.

Now I am a bachelor, I live with my son
And we work at the weaver's trade
And every, every time that I look into his eyes
He reminds me of that fair young maid:
He reminds me of that summer-time
And most of the winter too
And the many, many times that I held her in my arms
Just to save her from the foggy, foggy dew.

I have no doubt that this attractive number had its origin in the English countryside, but I sang it so often in the dim and distant days of my youth that I thought I should make a place for it.

12. Easy and Slow

Words and Music: Traditional, Dublin

'Twas down by christ church that I first met with An-nie, A neat lit-tle girl-and not a bit shy,— She told me her fath-er who came from Dun-gann-on, would take her back home in the sweet bye-and-bye, And what's that to a-ny man wheth-er or no wheth-er I'm a-isy or wheth-er I'm true — As I lift-ed her pet-ti-coat A-isy and slow and I tied up my sleeve for to buck-le her shoe.

From city or country a girl's a jewel
And well-made for gripping the most of them are
But any young fellow he is really a fool
If he tries at the first time to go a bit far.
 Chorus:

We wandered by Thomas Street down to the Liffey
The sunlight was gone and the evening grew dark
And along by Kingsbridge and begod in a jiffy
Me arm was around her beyond in the Park.
 Chorus:

Now if you should go the the town of Dungannon
You can search till your eyeballs are empty or blind
Be you sitting or walking or sporting or standing
A girl like Annie you never will find.
 Chorus:

I picked up this most attractive ballad from the singing of Henry Varian at his Brookside Village Inn in Boston when I was performing my one-man show there.

23

13. The Spanish Lady

Words and Music: Traditional

As I went down to Dub-lin City- at the hour of Twelve at night who should I see but a Span-ish lady- Wash-ing her feet by can-dle light first she wash'd them Then she dried them o-ver a fire of am-ber coals in all my life I ne'er did see a-maid so sweet a-bout the soul Whack-fol the too-ral- too-ra-lad-die whack-fol-the-too-ral-oo-ral-ay Whack-fol-the-too-ral- too-ra-lad-die whack-fol-the-too-ral-oo-ral-ay.

As I came back through Dublin city
At the hour of half past eight
Who should I spy but the Spanish Lady
Brushing her hair in the broad daylight;
First she tossed it, then she brushed it
On her lap was a silver comb
In all my life I ne'er did see
A maid so fair since I did roam.

As I went back through Dublin city
As the sun began to set
Who should I spy but the Spanish Lady
Catching a moth in a golden net
When she saw me then she fled me
Lifting her petticoat over her knee
In all my life I ne'er did see
A maid so shy as the Spanish Lady.

I've wandered north and I've wandered south
Through Stonybatter and Patrick's Close
Up and around the Gloster Diamond
And back by Napper Tandy's house
Old age has laid her hand on me
Cold as a fire of ashy coals
In all my life I ne'er did see
A maid so sweet as the Spanish Lady.

A lively song of uncertain, but probably Dublin, origin which was the favourite piece of my friend Dan Donovan at private ballad sessions late at night in the back room of the Group Theatre. 'Now we will sing,' Tom, the barman, would proclaim when all but the select few had been expelled.

14. The Zoological Gardens

Words and Music: Traditional, Dublin

Saturday night we had no dough
So I took the mot out to see the Zoo,
There were lions and tigers and kangaroos.
Inside the Zoological Gardens.

Well we went out there by Castleknock
Said she to me 'Will we court by the Lough'
Then I knew she was one of the rare old stock,
Inside the Zoological Gardens.

Said she to me, 'My dear friend Jack,
Sure, I'd like a ride on the elephant's back.'
Will ye get outa that or I'll give you such a crack,
Inside the Zoological Gardens.

We went out there on our honeymoon,
Said the mot to me, 'It you don't come soon,
I'll have to sleep with the hairy baboon,
Inside the Zoological Gardens.'

Another song taken down from the singing of Fergus Cahill at the Group Theatre. Completely Dublin in location but also in the nasal type of singing most suitable when delivering it.

25

15. The Garden where the Praties grow

Words and Music: Johnny Patterson

Have you ever been in love Boys or did you ever feel the pain I'd rather be in gaol myself than be in love again Tho' the girl I met was beautiful, I'd have you all to know that I met her in the garden where the praties grow.

Chorus:
She was just the sort of creature boys that nature did intend
To walk right thro' the world me boys without the Green Bend
Nor did she wear a chignon, I'd have you all to know
And I met her in the garden where the praties grow.
   Chorus

She was singing an ould Irish song called Gragal M'Cree,*
Oh, says I, what a wife she'd make for an Irish boy like me.
I was on important business, yet I didn't like to go,
And leave the girl or the garden where the praties grow.
   Chorus

Says I, 'My pretty fair maid I hope you'll pardon me,'
But she wasn't like those city girls that would say, 'You're making free,'
She answered me right modestly, and curtsied very low,
Saying you're welcome to the garden where the praties grow.
   Chorus

Sez I, 'My pretty colleen I am tired of single life.
And if you've no objections sure I'll make you my sweet wife.
Say she, 'I'll ask my parents, and tomorrow I'll let you know
If you meet me in the garden where the praties grow.'
   Chorus

Her parents they consented, and we're blessed with children three,
Two boys like their mother, and a girl the image of me.
And now I'm going to train them up the way they ought to go
For to dig in the garden where the praties grow.
Chorus

Johnny Patterson, king of the 'Free and Easies' was a circus clown and song writer. He was killed having been hit by an iron bar in the 1890s after a political meeting in Tralee. Harry Bradshaw, a Patterson fan and expert, with the assistance of Anthony H. Coxe of Devon has collected many of the songs.

* Gragal M'Cree (Geal Mo Chroide): bright love of my heart.

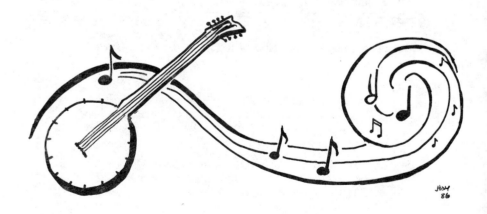

16. Biddy Donoghue

Words and Music: Johnny Patterson

It was in the County Kerry — Not far away from Clare — where the boys and girls are merry and children I declare —. The town is called Killorglin —. 'Tis a pretty place to view —, And what makes it interesting is my Biddy Donaghue — oh, Biddy Donaghue — I really do love you — Although I'm in America to you I will be true — Now Biddy Donaghue — I'll tell you what I'll do —, Just take the name of Paterson and I'll take Donaghue!

Our father is a farmer and a dacent man is he,
He's admired by all the people from Kilorglin to Tralee,
And Biddy on a Sunday when coming home from Mass;
Is admired by all the people so they stop to let her pass.

I sent her home a picture I did upon my word
It was't a picture of meself but of a great big bird;
It was the American eagle and says 'Miss Donahue,
The eagle's wings are large enough to shelter me and you.'

Another song, less well known than The Praties, *of Johnny Patterson, this came to me from the collection of the late Seán F. Healy.*

17. Three Lovely Lassies from Bannion

Words and Music: Traditional

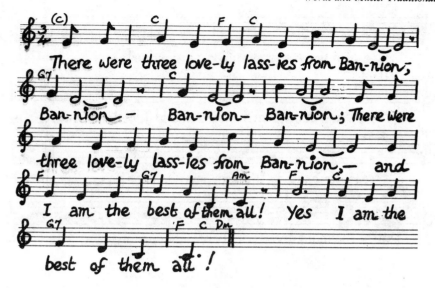

For me father has forty white shillin's, shillin's, shillin's, shillin's,
Me father has forty white shillin's
And the grass of a goat and a cow
And the grass of a goat and a cow.

And me mother says that I can marry, etc.,
And she'll lave me her bed when she dies, etc.

So I'm sendin' me shoes to be mended, etc.,
And me petticoat to be dyed green, etc.

And on next Sunday morning I'll meet him, etc.,
And I shall be dressed like a queen, etc.

Picked up from the singing of Delia Murphy many years ago. It was one of her best known numbers, delivered with the swing which lent so much to her voice.

18. Blow the Candle Out

Words and Music: Traditional

'Tis of a young apprentice came a courting of his dear The night being bright and shining and the stars being gazing clear He came to his love's window for to ease her of her pain The maid arose and barred the door and went to bed again

'Your mammy and your daddy
In yonder bed do lie
Embracing one another, love,
And why not you and I?
For when six months is over
And my 'Prentice time is out
I'll take you in my arms, love,
And blow the candle out.'

When six months they were over
Full six months and a day
He wrote her home a letter
That he was going away;
That he must do his duty
Like any soldier stout,
And he could ne'er return again
To blow the candle out.

Now this may be a warning
To all young maids like me,
Never trust a false young man
No matter what they say;
For when they're still apprentices
Before their time is out
They'll go away and leave their love
To blow the candle out.

What all good lovers do when the party's over. Based on the tune of an English Christmas Carol it appeared on a ballad sheet at least one hundred and sixty years ago. Another warning that young men may be deserters in more ways than one.

19. The Sweet Brown Knowe

Words and Music: Traditional

Come all ye lads and lasses and hear my mournful tale, Ye tender hearts that weep for love to sigh you will not fail, Tis all about a young man and my song will tell you how He lately came a courtin' of the Maid of the Sweet Brown Knowe.

Said he, 'My pretty fair maid, will you come along with me,
We'll both go off together, and married we will be;
We'll join hands in wedlock bans, I'm speaking to you now,
And I'll do my best endeavour for the Maid of the Sweet Brown Knowe.'

This fair and fickle young thing she knew not what to say;
Her eyes did shine like silver bright and merrily did play.
She said, 'Young man, your love subdue, for I am not ready now,
And I'll spend another season at the foot of the Sweet Brown Knowe.'

Said he, 'my pretty fair maid, how can you say so,
Look down on yonder valley, where my crops do gently grow;
Look down on yonder valley, where my horses and my plough
Are at their daily labour for the Maid of the Sweet Brown Knowe.'

'If they're at their daily labour, kind sir, it's not for me;
For I've heard of your behaviour, I have indeed,' said she.
'There is an inn where you call in, I have heard the people say,
Where you rap and call and pay for all, and go home at the break of day.'

'If I rap and call and pay for all, the money is all my own;
And I'll never spend your fortune, for I hear you have got none
You thought you had my poor heart broke, in talking with me now,'
And I left her where I found her at the foot of the Sweet Brown Knowe.

Originating from the north but once popular all over the country – how to treat a reluctant sweetheart. An attractive tune for an attractive party piece.

20. Kitty O'Toole

Words and Music: Arranged by Seán F. Healy
Collected by James N. Healy

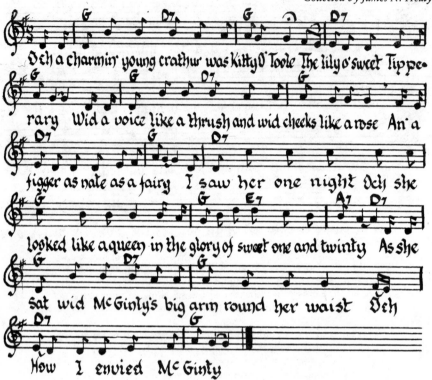

Och a charmin' young crathur was Kitty O'Toole The lily o' sweet Tipperary Wid a voice like a thrush and wid cheeks like a rose An' a
figger as nate as a fairy I saw her one night Och she
looked like a queen in the glory of sweet one and twinty As she
sat wid McGinty's big arm round her waist Och
How I envied McGinty

Six months after that on a sweet summer's day,
The boys and the girls were invited
By Mickey O'Toole of the cabin beyant,
To see Kate and McGinty united.
An' when in the church they were made into wan,
And the priest gave them blessings in plenty,
As she sat wid McGinty's big arm round her waist,
Och, how I envied McGinty!

But the years have gone by, and McGinty is dead:
Shure me heart was all bruk up with pity.
I see her so lonely, and mournful, and sad,
An' I went and got married to Kitty.
But now when I look where McGinty is laid,
Wid a stone o'er his head cold and flinty;
As he lies there so peaceful an' quiet and still –
Oh! how I envy McGinty!

Here it worked out all too well! One is reminded of the old music-hall song Lucky Jim *by this ballad from the collection left to me by the late Seán F. Healy from his extensive repertory.*

21. The Stuttering Lovers

Words and Music: Traditional

Then out came the bonny wee lass
And she was O! so fair
And she went into the poor man's corn
To see if the birds were th-th-th-th-th-there, my lads,
To see if the birds were there.

And out came the brave young lad
And he was a fisherman's son
And he went into the poor man's corn
To see where the lass has g-g-g-g-g-gone, my lads,
To see where the lass had gone.

He put his arm around her waist
He kissed her cheek and chin
Then out spake the bonny wee lass
'I fear it is a s-s-s-s-s-sin, my lad,
I fear it is a sin.'

He kissed her once and he kissed her twice
And he kissed her ten times o'er
'Twas fine to be kissing that bonny wee lass
That never was kissed bef-f-f-f-fore, my lads,
That never was kissed before.

Then out came the poor old man
And he was tattered and torn
'Faith if that's the way ye're minding the corn
I'll mind it myself in the m-m-m-m-m-morning,' he said,
'I'll mind it myself in the morn.'

Pity the lover who got into trouble because he couldn't p-p-p-pop the question: and perhaps the girl who got into trouble because she couldn't say n-n-n-no fast enough.
    Probably of Scottish origin.

22. I was told by My Aunt

Words and Music: Traditional

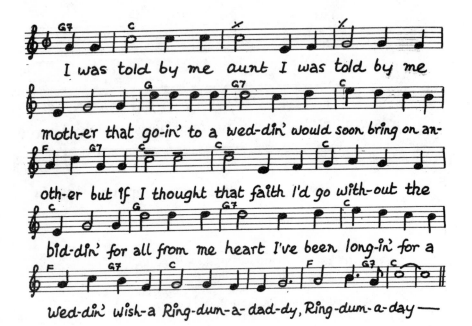

I was told by me aunt I was told by me
moth-er that go-in' to a wed-din' would soon bring on an-
oth-er but if I thought that faith I'd go with-out the
bid-din' for all from me heart I've been long-in' for a
wed-din' wish-a Ring-dum-a-dad-dy, Ring-dum-a-day —

My sister Annie, – and she's younger than I am
She has so many sweethearts she's goin' to deny 'em
But here's to meself faith I haven't got so many
But, oh, through my heart I'd be thankful for any.

And my sister Ellen, and she's not yet forsaken
At the age of seventeen a bride she was taken
At the age of nineteen she had a son and daughter
But I'm sweet forty-five and I never had an offer.

Come mencemen, come pencemen, come tinkers and come tailors
Come fiddler, come fifer; come sailors and come w'avers
Come ragman, come bagman; come foolish and come witty
Don't let me die an old maid – yisha, marry me for pity.

And now to conclude I give thanks to a neighbour
Who introduced me to a black chimney-sweeper
He says that he loves me, and swears that he will keep me
And I'll be happy with me black chimney sweeper.

One of the best numbers collected by the late and great Delia Murphy but not as well remembered as some of the others. What life she gave to her singing: not operatic quality, but, lord, how effective!

23. The High Heel'd Shoes

Words and Music: Tade Gowran
Collected from Mike Sheedy, Lyracroumpane

From London and France they bring music and dance, and in fashion they dress the hat
'Tis the divils delight to see them at night when they're dancin' the fox's trot
But mavrone, to be sure, 'tis bad to be poor, but poverty's no excuse;
For the Divil may care, but they're bobbing their hair; and they're wearing those
high-heeled shoes.

But I pause to say that the other day I met with a Cailín deas
She was worn and thin, with a rawny old skin, and her face like a tinker's ass.
I saluted *Lá Breagh*, but she cocked up her jaw, and was off like a hatching goose
I could plainly see the skirt of her knee, and she was wearing those high-heeled shoes.

For I pity the man who's married to wan of those slippery useless heels
They spends half the day a-makin' the tay, and thinkin' of jigs and reels,
And his dear darling wife will threaten his life for the orders he don't obey
And he'll curse the day he met a *laká* with those terrible high-heeled shoes.

'Tis no wonder at all the lightning would fall and destruction is drawing nigh
The clergy complain, but they talks all in vain, whether speaking to girl or boy
But let each man dear from far or near a sensible wife now choose,
Let him fix for a wife that will brighten his life, and to Hell with those high-heeled shoes!

Written by Tade Gowran and collected from Mike Sheedy of Lyracroumhane one evening among the mists of that remote place in delightful company.

24. The Moonshiner

Words and Music: Traditional, nineteenth century

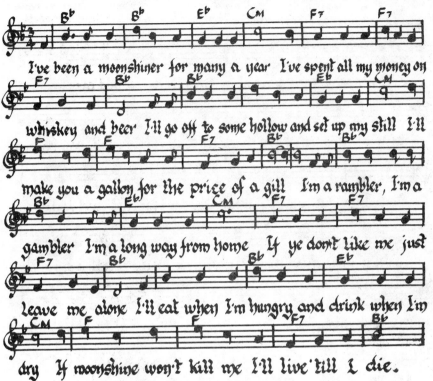

I've been a moonshiner for many a year I've spent all my money on whiskey and beer I'll go off to some hollow and set up my still I'll make you a gallon for the price of a gill I'm a rambler, I'm a gambler I'm a long way from home If ye don't like me just leave me alone I'll eat when I'm hungry and drink when I'm dry If moonshine won't kill me I'll live 'till I die.

I'll go to some hollow in this country,
Ten gallons of wash and I'll go on the spree;
No woman to follow and the world will be mine –
I love none so well as I love the moonshine.
   Chorus

Moonshine, dear moonshine, oh, how I love thee –
Ye kilt me poor father, but don't you try me;
Bless all moonshiners and bless all moonshine
It's breath is as sweet as the dew on the vine.
   Chorus

There's moonshine for Molly and moonshine for May,
Moonshine for my love and she'll sing all the day;
Moonshine for breakfast and moonshine for me tay,
Moonshine, O me hearties; it's moonshine for me!
   Chorus

Moonshine is another name for Poitín, *the national but highly illegal beverage of the Emerald Isle. Being illegal, a drop of the 'Craythur' is therefore much sought after. Look out, however, it is a dangerous medicine.*

25. The Rale Oul' Mountain Dew

Words and Music: Traditional

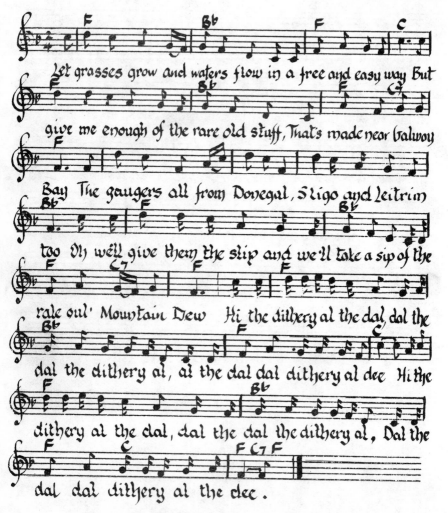

Let grasses grow and waters flow in a free and easy way But give me enough of the rare old stuff, That's made near Galway Bay The gaugers all from Donegal, Sligo and Leitrim too Oh well give them the slip and we'll take a sip of the rale oul' Mountain Dew Hi the dithery al the dal, dal the dal the dithery al, al the dal dal dithery al dee Hi the dithery al the dal, dal the dal the dithery al, Dal the dal dal dithery al the dee.

At the foot of the hill there's a neat little still
  Where the smoke curls up to the sky;
By a whiff of the smell you can plainly tell
  That there's poitín, boys, close by.
For it fills the air with a perfume rare,
  And betwixt both me and you,
As home we roll, we can drink a bowl
  Or a bucketful of mountain dew.

38

Now learned men who use the pen,
  Have wrote the praises high
Of the sweet poitín from Ireland green
  Distilled from wheat and rye.
Away will pills, it will cure all ills,
  Of the Pagan, Christian or Jew;
So take off your coat and grease your throat
  With the real old mountain dew.

Yet another name for the 'Wicked Potion'; and a reminder of the days in this cheerful song when the 'Gangerman' was the foe of the illicit distillers. Amazing how many songs are written in Ireland about drink: we must have a liking for the stuff. Father Mathew had an uphill job.

26. The Poitín Song

Words and Music: Collected from Seán Lahane of Ballyvourney

Oh come all you lads and lassies fair, attend to my oration I
hope you'll hear me in my song and give me an ovation I
now intend your voices and your kind consideration to
wish me joy and happiness in exporting transportation agus
gheobham arís an crúiscín is bíodh sé lán Grá mo chroí mo
chruiscín, sláinte geal mo bhúirnín Gheobham arís an
cruiscín is bíodh sé lán agus grá mo chroí mo

39

chruiscín is bíodh sé lán.

It was in the month of June or so, some cowardly hearted traitor
He went into the barracks and his story there related;
He said that in that Western glen far, far out in the mountain,
There was a poitín Irish still flowing from a crystal fountain.
  Chorus

It was early the next morning the police made preparations.
They hired a car and driver for to take them to the Station:
But when they reached the shanty they found they were mistaken,
There was neither manufacturer, or anything relating.
  Chorus

Now this crystal dropped right from the still, 'twould cure all kinds of ailments,
'Twould cure the yalla jaunders, the scarletine and measles;
Twould banish heart diseases, from your lungs 'twould drive flemation
From your soul 'twould drive the divil, from your heart 'twould drive temptation.
  Chorus

Now the Christmas (Easter) is approaching, boys, we're in a consternation,
We don't know where to get a drop without adulteration
Our Irish manufacture is the finest in the nation
Because it is distributed without duty or taxation.
  Chorus

And now to conclude and finish – and I hope I've spoke no treason
Freedom is soon dawning, and we'll have Home Rule sa 'Ghaeltacht'
We'll banish all land grabbers, and cowardly hearted traitors
And we'll have our poitín Irish still ansúd gan Bhuíochas d'éinne!
  Chorus

*I heard Seán Lehane of Ballyvourney sing this bilingual song at a 'Tops of the Town' performance
in Macroom some eight years ago and he was kind enough to give me a copy of the words and music.*

27. The Black Stripper

Words and Music: Colm Ó Lochlainn
Collected from 'Micilín the Monks'

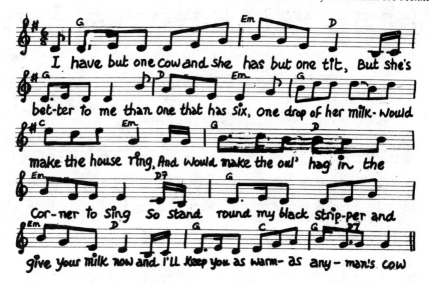

I have but one cow and she has but one tit, But she's
bet-ter to me than one that has six, One drop of her milk would
make the house ring, And would make the oul' hag in the
Cor-ner to sing So stand round my black strip-per and
give your milk now and I'll keep you as warm as any man's cow

Ten acres I hold and ten acres I plough,
And all that it grows goes to the black cow,
If I can but feed her a gallon of ale,
To give a wee drapple she never will fail.
    So stand round. . .

I have four stacks of barley that I must knock down,
In forty-eight hours I will have them ground,
I'll bottle my stripper and bring her to town,
And if I meet the gauger, I will knock him down.
    So, stand round. . .

Being illegal, the contraption from which poitín is made has to go under another name. As a cow gives milk, the collection of tubes, pots and pieces of metal which distill the potion is called the black stripper. An old song of the west collected by Colm Ó Lochlainn from an old man known as 'Micilín the Monks' over sixty years ago.

28. The Ballyhooley Blue Ribbon Army

Words and Music: Robert Martin

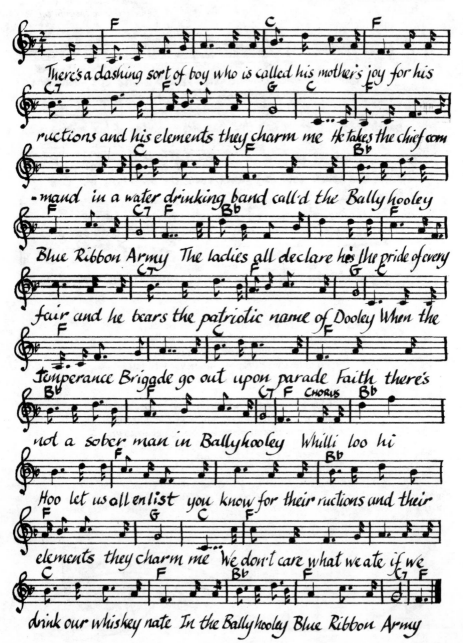

There's a dashing sort of boy who is called his mother's joy for his ructions and his elements they charm me He takes the chief command in a water drinking band call'd the Ballyhooley Blue Ribbon Army The ladies all declare he's the pride of every fair and he bears the patriotic name of Dooley When the temperance Brigade go out upon parade Faith there's not a sober man in Ballyhooley Whilli loo hi Hoo let us all enlist you know for their ructions and their elements they charm me We don't care what we ate if we drink our whiskey nate In the Ballyhooley Blue Ribbon Army

When we're out upon patrol, and we're under his control,
We take, of course, a most extended radius;
Although it's very clear we drink only ginger beer,
We find the drinking sometimes rather tadius;
The polis one fine day, faith they chanced to come our way,
And they said we were behaving most unruly,
When the sergeant he did state that we were not walking straight,
Faith, we stretched him for a corpse in Ballyhooley.

Then before the magistrate everyone of us did state,
That we had taken nothing that could injure;
And as it's very clear we drink only ginger beer,
There must have been some stingo in the ginger.
Some of us did own we were drinking zoedone,
But the polis was behaving most unruly;
It was all of no avail, and within the county jail,
Lies the temperance brigade of Ballyhooley.

There's a moral to my song, and it won't detain ye long,
Give up strong drink of every description,
And as it's very clear ye may tire of ginger beer,
I'll give you all a temperance prescription:
First the sugar you have got, then the water bilin' hot,
And the limon, faith you'll find I'm spaking truly,
And the way you'd sprinkle salt, toss a glass or two of malt;
Faith they call it limonade in Ballyhooley.

Encore verse
As you've kindly said encore, faith; well here's a trifle more, –
One mornin' patriotic Captain Dooley,
Oh, looking gay and nice, with his nightcap full of ice,
Appears upon parade in Ballyhooley.
Says he, 'Boys, do not think that my headache's caused thro' drink,
And to prove to ye that I am spakin' truly,
Just to show I'm not afraid, produce the limonade,
Begorra! we'll have another dose of Ballyhooley.

Robert Martin, who wrote the song, was brother of Violet Martin, who, as Martin Ross, wrote the delightful shows about the Irish R.M. with Edith Œ. Somerville. Edith was of the opinion that Martin was a much better song-maker than Percy French whom they knew. He wasn't of course, but this is a good song.

29. Old Rosin the Bow

Words: American-Irish traditional 1838; completed by James N. Healy
Music: Éogan Cóir

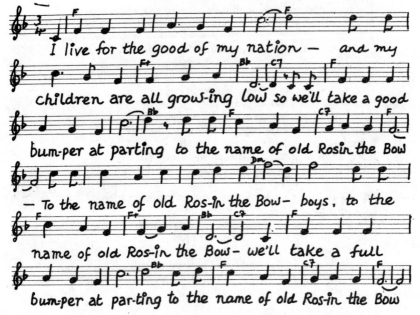

I live for the good of my nation — and my

children are all grow-ing low so we'll take a good

bum-per at parting to the name of old Rosin the Bow

— To the name of old Ros-in the Bow — boys, to the

name of old Ros-in the Bow — we'll take a full

bum-per at par-ting to the name of old Ros-in the Bow

In the gay round of pleasure I've travelled
And I won't leave behind any foe
So while my companions are jovial
They will drink to old Rosin the Bow.

> They will drink to old Rosin the Bow
> They will drink to old Rosin the Bow
> While my companions are jovial
> They will drink to old Rosin the Bow.

So when I'm laid out on the bed boys
You'll hear my voice calling so low
Will you send down a barrel of porter
For the sake of old Rosin the Bow.

> For the sake of old Rosin the Bow, etc.

Then get half a dozen fine boozers
And line them all up in a row
And fill 'em with pints to remember
They once drank to old Rosin the Bow.

> They once drank with Rosin the Bow etc.

44

Then dig a big hole in the meadow
With a bottle at head and at toe
To teach all my friends to remember
To drink to old Rosin the Bow.

To drink to old Rosin the Bow, etc.

This old song was known in America even before Famine times; although it was almost without doubt of either Scottish or Irish origin – probably the latter because of the univeral use of the tune 'Eogan Cóir'. I have used some of the very old lyrics and the remainder from verses used at ballad sessions in the Group Theatre in the 1960.
    Rosin liked his tipple too.

30. The Agricultural Irish Girl

Words: This version collected by James N. Healy
Music: Traditional

If all the girls in Ir-e-land were gath-ered up to-gether There's

No wan like my Mary Ann in e-ve-ry kind of wea-ther The

rain won't wash the pow-der off her face-she doesn't wear it,and her

fig-ure and face are all her own the truth I must declare it. She's a

fine stout lump of an ag-er-a-cul-chur-il Irish girl; Her

face is worth a for-tune and her figure is all her own. She can

Strike that hard you would think you were hit by the

Kick of a mule, but the full of a house of

Irish love is Mar-y Ann Mal-one ____

45

She was never e-d-i-cated,
She doesn't know her letters,
But she's all a lady wants, me boys,
And better than her betters.
She doesn't speak Ital-i-an
Or read the sporting papers;
But she knows the horse will win the race –
She knows the form, be japers.

She was only seventeen last year
But still she's growing greatly;
I wonder what her form will be
When she fills it out complately
You'd think your hand was in a vice
The minute that she'd take it,
And if there's any cake at hand
'Tis Mary Ann will ate it.

I picked up in the far distant 1940s when, as youths, we used to go to race meetings. Colm Ó Lochlainn had a somewhat different version, or remembrance of the lady who used to sing it; but she was a well remembered character.

31. Goodbye Mursheen Durkin

Words and Music: Colm Ó Lochlainn

In the days I went a-courtin' I was never tired re-sortin' to the ale-house and the play-house and many a house beside, But I told me brother Seámus I'll be off now and grow famous and before I come home again I'll roam the world wide

Oh! I courted girls in Blarney,
In Kanturk and Killarney,
In Passage and in Queenstown, I mean the Cove of Cork;
But I'm tired of all this pleasure,
So now I'll take my leisure,
And the next time that you hear, 'twill be a letter from New York.

So goodbye Mursheen Durkin,
Sure, I'm sick and tired of workin',
No more I'll dig the praties, no longer I'll be fooled:
But sure as my name is Corney
I'll be off to Californey
And instead of diggin' praties, I'll be diggin' lumps of goold.

My friend the late Colm Ó Lochlainn, who was collecting ballads when most people had forgotten about them said to me in what was I think my last conversation with him, 'I don't mind people using ballads from my books, but you'd think they'd give me an acknowledgement for taking them,' and instanced the use of this number which had revived in popularity at the time. He was one of the greatest collectors in the field.

47

32. The Little Beggarman

Words and Music: Traditional, Dublin

I slept in a barn one night in Currabawn,
A shocking wet night it was but I slept until the dawn;
There was holes in the roof and the rain drops coming through,
And the rats and the cats were all playing peek-a-boo.
Who did I waken but the woman of the house,
With her white-spotted apron and her fine gingham blouse;
She began to get excited and all I said was 'Boo
Sure don't be afraid at all, 'tis only Johnny Dhu.'

I met a little girl when a-walking out one day,
'Good morrow, little flaxen-haired girl,' I did say;
'Good morrow, little beggarman, and how do you do?
With your rags and your tags and your ould rigadoo.'
I'll buy a pair of leggin's, and a collar and a tie,
And a nice young lady I'll go courting by-and-bye;
I'll buy a pair of goggles and I'll colour them with blue,
And an ould-fashioned lady I will make her too.

So all along the high road with my bag upon my back,
Over the fields with my bulgin' heavy sack;
With holes in my shoes and my toes a peeping through,
Singing skill-a-malick-adoodle with my ould rigadoo,
Oh! I must be going be bed, for it's getting late at night,
The fire's all raked and now 'tis out the light;
For now you've heard the story of my ould rigadoo,
So good-bye and God be with you, from ould Johnny Dhu.

A Dublin song remembered from the singing of Fergus Cahill during ballad sessions at the Group Theatre in the 1960s.

33. The Bradys of Kilanne

Words and Music: Traditional

When I went down to the iron bridge the place they called the Strand 'Twas there I hired for seven long years with the Bradys of Kilanne, The morning that I hired with him 'Twas plainly I could see, He promised me eggs and bacon And he then shook hands with me Saying you're welcome to my house Johnny, O you're with a dacent man 'Twas little I knew! had to deal with the Bradys of Kilanne.

When I woke up in the mornin' I heard a terrible row,
'Twas the gettin' up of Brady, or the gruntin' of a sow
'Hurry up there with the water, make a sup of tay for Nan'
'Twas ever and all the same old call with the Bradys of Kilanne.

When I got out on the farm my hair grew like a wig
My coat it got too small for me, my trousers got too big
I'm sending for Micky Hennessy, he'll be on now soon with the van
To handcap me to the County Home from the Bradys of Kilanne.

When I went into bed at night, 'twas loudly I did bawl;
The fleas they made a strong attack, my kidneys for the haul.
With scratching and with tearing, my skin grew like a tan
I roared and bawled and kicked the walls at the Bradys of Kilanne.

A spailpín song. Kilanne is about six miles from Ballybunion in north Kerry. I often heard John B. Keane singing snatches of it, and eventually, from him and others, I got what is near to the full version.

50

34. Aloysius Alphonsus O'Leary

Words: James N. Healy
Music: Adaptation of 'The Black Velvet Band'

I started the round of the festivals in Ireland so green and so free I tasted oysters in Galway and gaped at the Rose of Tralee I was deafened by opera in Wexford I angled for shark down in Cove But there'd be one fellow before me no matter where ever I'd rove And his eyes would be shining like diamonds He'd barely be able to stand Aloysius Alphonsus O'Leary with a bottle of stout in his hand.

We'd travel from Dublin to Waterford, by Sligo, Athlone and Tralee
And there he'd be landed before us, by Shannon, or Liffey or Lee.
I would change my transport from railroad to bus, and to steamer and air
But tho' he'd be hitching and thumbing a lift, before me he'd always be there.   *Chorus:*

The ballads would ring to the roof-tops, about Ireland's lovely land,
Or going to join the IRA, or the girl with the Black Velvet Band.
They would sing of Boolavogue's glory, or the fabulous Boys of Fair Hill
And there he'd be leading the chorus, and rapidly drinking his fill.   *Chorus:*

Now come all ye lads of this nation, and a warning take from me,
If you're making the rounds of the Festivals, some faces you always will see.
They may not be always invited, but be sure they'll be always at hand,
They'll be drinking your porter, and pinching your girl
And untying her Black Velvet Band! *Chorus:*

Written at the last moment for a show at the Group Theatre in Cork in 1967 and performed the following night. Inspired by party followers who seek booze and birds at festivals rather than 'Culchure'.

35. I Sing of Lies

Words and Music: Traditional: translated by James N. Healy
from 'Amhrán na mBréag'

'Twas a fun-ny old thing that I saw by the
road-side, an eel with his bag-pipes was
play-ing a tune and the trout in the pool by his
side had his shoes on and was tap-ping his
feet by the light of the moon man-ga-lum
did-e-ro, shuff-le and prance and it's up on your
trot-ters and join in the dance

There's a sheep futtin' turf in the bog with a skylark
Who is storing the turf in the beard of a goose
While a water-hen's playing a tune on the jew's harp
And the fox by the fireside is having a snooze.

52

The crow on the hillside is gathering lettuce
While the parson's old horse is out bagging the meal ('male')
The hen and the drake took a passage to Turkey
And on.board is a hare drinking pints of strong ale.

The Red Rose I plucked had no prickle or thorn
I hope to believe me you never will fail
For the Church is down dancing a jig in the valley
And you'd be worse than I if you swallow my tale.

A new translation of an old Irish song, popular in its type at once time, when one outrageous statement follows another.

35a. Amhrán na mBréag

Words and Music: Traditional

Is greannúr an ní seo do chím-se ar na bóithribh,
Eascú agus píob aici 'sior-sheinim cheóil dúinn,
An breac lughach 'sa' linn – och! ba mhín iad a bhróga,
Is an bhfeacúir na caoire 'sa' gheimhre 'buaint mhóna?
Cursa:

Da bhfeicfeá-sa bricín a' breith coinín i bpoll leis,
Is nead ag an bhfuiseóg i bhféasóg an ghanndail,
Ceard uisge 'cronán 's a' buaint ceóil bhreá as trompaí
'Gus madarua ar an dteinteán is an sraoileán ag amhastruigh.
Cursa:

Dá bhfeicfeá-sa an fhionnóg ar stuaic a' buaint biolair,
Is Garrán na mBráthar le n-a chárt a' tomhas mine,
An chearc is an bárdal idir an Spáinneach 's an Turcaigh
'Gus goirae agus bríste air ag ól fíona ar bórd luinge.
Chorus:

Do chonnac-sa sgeacha gan mhaidí gan deilgne,
Dhá mhadarua is iad gan chluasa gan earball,
Teampall ar fuiad gleannta is é a' damhas is ag eiteallaigh,
Is ní bréagaí mé féinigh ná an té seo do chreidfeadh mé!
Chorus:

The original lyric in Irish of the above.

36. The Mad Puck Goat

Words: Translation by James N. **Healy**
Music: 'An Poc ar **Buile**'

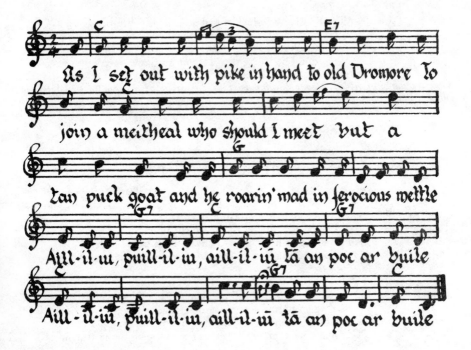

As I set out with pike in hand to old Dromore To
join a meitheal who should I meet but a
tan puck goat and he roarin' mad in ferocious mettle
Aill-il-iu, puill-il-iu, aill-il-iu tā an poc ar buile
Aill-il-iu, puill-il-iu, aill-il-iu tā an poc ar buile

He chased me over bush and weed
And through the bog the run proceeded
'Till he caught his horns in a clump of gorse
And on his back I jumped unheeded.
   Chorus:

There was ne'er a rock with no passage through
Which he didn't jump, and me like Eddie Macken
But when he lepped clean down Faill Breach
I felt like a load of old wet sackin'.
   Chorus:

When the sergeant stood in Rochestown
With a force of guards to apprehend us
The goat he tore his tousers down
And made rags of his breeches and new suspenders.
   Chorus:

In Dingle the following afternoon
The parish priest came to call us to order
And he swore from the pulpit each Sunday in June
'Twas the divil on the back of his old grandfather.
Chorus:

My translation of the song, from the Coolea region, made popular in the Irish version by Seán Ó Sé.

36a. An Poc Ar Buile

Words and Music: Traditional

Ar mo dhul dom siar chun Droichead Uí Mhórdha,
Píce im dhóid is mé ag dul i meitheal,
Cé chasfail orm i gcumar ceoidh
Ach pocán crón is é ar buile.

Curfa:
Aillilliú, puilliliú, alliliú, tá an poc ar buile,
Aillilliú, puilliliú, alliliú, tá an poc ar buile,

Do ritheamar trasna trí ruilleogach
Is do ghluais an comhrac ar fud na muinge,
Is treascairt dá bhfuair se sna turtóga,
Chuas ina ainneaoin ar a dhroim le fuinneamh.
Curfa:

Níor fhág sé carraig go raibh scót ann
Ná gur rith le fórsa chun mé a mhilleadh,
Is ea ansan do chaith sé an léim ba mhó
Le fána mór na Faille Brice.
Curfa:

Bhí garda mór i mBaile an Róistigh
Is bhailigh fórsaí chun sinn a chlipeadh,
Do bhuail sé rop dá adhairc sa tóin air
Is dá bhristi nua do dhein sé giobail.
Curfa:

I nDaingean uí Chúise le haghaidh an tráthnóna
Bhí an sagart paróiste amach inár gcoinnibh,
Is é dúirt gurbh é an diabhal ba dhóigh leis
A ghaibh an treo ar phocán buile.
Curfa:

37. Do You want your Old Lobby washed down?

Words and Music: Traditional

I've a nice lit-tle cot and a good bit of land and a
place by the side of the sea — and I cares a-bout
no wan be-cause I be-lieves that there's no-bo-dy
cares a-bout me — me peace is de-stroy'd and I'm
fair-ly an-noy'd by a las-sie who works in the town she
calls ev'ry day as she pas-ses me way: Do you
CHORUS
want yer oul' lob-by wash'd down — Do you
want yer oul' lob-by wash'd down, Con Shine, Do you
want yer oul' lob-by wash'd down ——

When he called for the rent the landlord was spent
When I told him no money I had
Besides 'twastn't fair to ask me to pay
For the times were so terribly bad,
He felt discontent at not getting his rent,
And he shook his big head in a frown,
Says he, 'I'll take half.' 'So,' says I with a laugh,
'Do you want your old lobby washed down?'

Now the boys look so bashful when they are out courtin'
They seem to look ever so shy
Sure to kiss a young maid, why they seem half afraid
But they would if they could on the sly.
But me I do things in a different way,
I don't give a nod or a frown
When I goes to court, I says, 'Here goes, old sport,
"Do you want your old lobby washed down?"'

*A song of obscure Cork origin – probably from the last century when people sometimes paid off **part** of their rent by cleaning the halls or outside part of the premises for the landlord.*

'DO YOU
WANT
YOUR
OLD
LOBBY
WASHED
DOWN
?'

Ham
86.

38. The Calabar

Words: Collected from Jean Pitts (1962)
Music: 'Limerick is Beautiful'

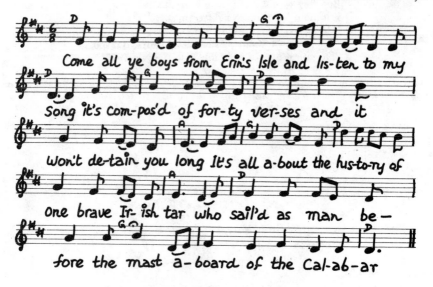

Come all ye boys from Erin's Isle and lis-ten to my
Song it's com-pos'd of for-ty ver-ses and it
won't de-tain you long It's all a-bout the his-to-ry of
one brave Ir-ish tar who sail'd as man before the mast a-board of the Cal-ab-ar

The Calabar was a clipper ship
Copper fastened both fore and aft;
The rudder was away behind
The wheel a great-big shaft.
With half a gale to swell her sail
She could do one knot an hour,
The fastest craft on the River Lee
She was only one donkey power.

The captain was a strapping youth
His height being four foot two.
His eyes were red, his ears were green,
His nose was a Prussian blue.
He wore a leather medal he won in the Zulu War.
And his wife was cook, pilot and crew
On board of the Calabar.

As we went down by the Holy Ground
The stormy wind did blow,
Our bosun slipped on an orange peel
And fell in the hold below.
The captain cried, 'A piratical junk
And on us she do gain,
And if ever I go to Spike again
Be japers I'll go be train.'

58

Now when we rounded Roches Point –
A very dangerous part –
Our ship she struck a knob of coal
Which wasn't marked on the chart.
To stop the vessel from sinking
And save our precious lives
We threw the cargo overboard
Including the captain's wife.

We got out our ammunition to
Meet the treacherous foe,
We had boarding pikes and
Cutlasses, and a rolling pin also,
'Put on full speed,' the captain said,
'Or we'll be sorely pressed
But do not shoot the engineer,
For he is doing his best.'

Oh, the heroes fell both thick and fast,
And pints of blood were spilt,
They were mostly falling before they
Were hit, in case they might be kilt.
And at last the pirate surrendered his ship
The crew being all flat out
And we found she was a sister ship,
With a cargo of Murphy's stout.

The ship is in Haulbowline now,
And the crew in the county jail;
And I'm the one surviving
Yet, to tell the terrible tale.
But if I could get back the ship
I'd be sailing off afar,
Of the whole bloody fleet I'd be
Admiral, in charge of the Calabar.

The Cruise of the Calabar *was originally a canal song. This version, given to me by John and Jean Pitts many moons ago was an adaptation to the open sea, or at any rate to the confines of Cork harbour.*

39. When Bananas grow on Gaslamps in Blackpool

Words and Music: The Warblers

When go-ing home the other night I saw a most am-az-ing sight, I saw ban-an-as grow-ing on gas-lamps in Black-pool one could sam-ple a good deal 'a bad pot-een from Inch-i-gee-la to see Ban-an-as grow on gas-lamps in Black-pool we were not drunk since this day month, and Pussy-foot is now out stunt we go home ve-ry so-ber as a rule — oh Pad-dy Flah-er-ty what hor-rid sights you made us See; Ban-an-as grow-ing on Gas-lamps in Black-pool

We have lots of work this year, and Pana Huts will disappear,
If Bananas grow on gaslamps in Blackpool,
Tons of work for labour skilled, and Patrick Street we shall rebuild,
When Bananas grow on gaslamps in Blackpool.
Builder's prices are knocked silly,
By Wilde from Piccadilly.
So spacious homes for workers soon we'll see.
A bath in each house I'll go bail
For the kids their little ships to sail.
When Bananas grow on gaslamps in Blackpool.

We get some hot stuff in the Pictures which escapes the Censor's strictures
Since Bananas grow on gaslamps in Blackpool.
But the Censors now we hope will use a stronger Periscope
When Bananas grow on gaslamps in Blackpool.
Picture houses too, I hear will all be swept out once a year
And the carpets fumigated now and then.
And Keatings Powder by the ton
Will make the little Jumpers run
When Bananas grow on gaslamps in Blackpool.

To get a County Council job you must have Irish in your Gob
Since Thaw-go-breag and Cunnis-thaw-thu is the rule.
But if the job is snug and fat all you'll want is Bannact leath.
Till Bananas grow on gaslamps in Blackpool.
You must get a thorough knowledge of Irish in a College
If a scavenger or stone-breaker you will be.
But. . . if Dhun and Dhorus you can't spell
A couple of cousins will do as well.
To vote you in to any job in Cork Cit-ee.

A popular Pierrot group in Cork during the years 1916-29 were the Warblers, and this was one of their most popular effusions. Dan Hobbs, a member of the troup, was a popular Cork comedian for many years. 'Periscope' was a picture critic. Patrick Street was in ruins from the burning by the 'Tans'. Fleas were well-known 'hosts' in some cinemas – such as one called the Imperial. Rules for employment may still be the same.

40. A Cork from out a Bottle

Words: Dan Hobbs
Music: Traditional

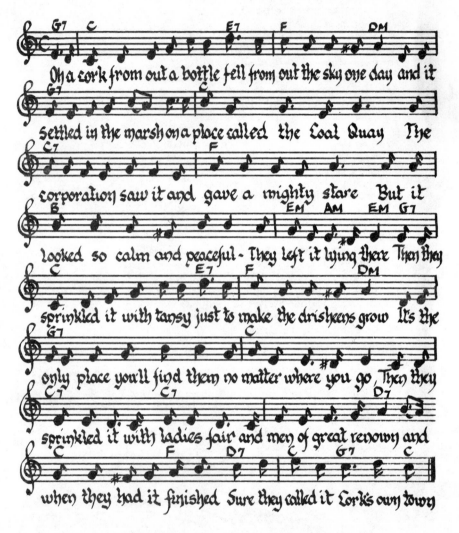

Oh a cork from out a bottle fell from out the sky one day and it
settled in the marsh on a place called the Coal Quay The
corporation saw it and gave a mighty stare But it
looked so calm and peaceful - They left it lying there Then they
sprinkled it with tansy just to make the drisheens grow It's the
only place you'll find them no matter where you go, Then they
sprinkled it with ladies fair and men of great renown and
when they had it finished Sure they called it Cork's own town

A parody on an old sentimental song, by Dan Hobbs, favourite with 'The Warblers'.

41. The Old Woman from Wexford

Words and Music: Traditional

There was an old wo-man in Wex-ford who in
Wex-ford town did dwell she lov'd her hus-band
dear-ly but an-other — man twice as well with me
rum-tum-tid-ill-ee dar-um and me rum-tum-tid-ill-ee dee—

One day she went to the doctor
Some medicine for to find
Saying, 'Doctor, give us something
That'll make me oul' man blind.' *Chorus:*

'Will ya feed him eggs and marrow bones
And make him suck them all
And it won't be so very long after
Till he won't see you at all.' *Chorus:*

The doctor wrote a letter
Aye, he signed with his hand
And he sent it off to the old man
So that he would understand. *Chorus:*

So she fed him eggs and marrow bones
And made him suck them all
And it wasn't so very long after
Till he couldn't see the wall. *Chorus:*

'Oh,' says he, 'I'd go and drown meself,
But that would be a sin.'
Says she, 'I'll go along with you
And I'll help to push you in.' *Chorus:*

The old woman, she stood back a bit
To get a running go,
The old man quickly stepped aside
And she went in below. *Chorus:*

O, how loudly did she roar,
And how loudly did she bawl,
'Arra hould your whist ould woman,' says he,
'Sure I can't see you at all.'   *Chorus:*

She swam and swam and swam and swam
Till she came to the further brim
The old man got a long larch pole
And he pushed her further in.   *Chorus:*

So eggs are eggs and marrow bones
May make your old man blind
But if you'd be sure to drown him
You must creep up close behind.   *Chorus:*

An old party song which exists in various versions. The effect of being able to 'join in' on such songs
made them popular in the communal ballad sessions which began to develop some twenty years ago.

42. The Wild Rover

Words and Music: Traditional

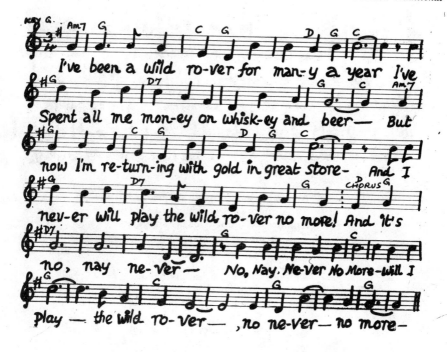

I've been a wild ro-ver for man-y a year I've
Spent all me mon-ey on whisk-ey and beer— But
now I'm re-turn-ing with gold in great store—And I
nev-er will play the wild ro-ver no more! And it's
no, nay ne-ver— No, Nay. Ne-ver No More—will I
Play — the wild ro-ver— ,no ne-ver— no more—

I went to an ale house I used to frequent,
And I told the landlady me money was spent,
I asked her for credit; she answered me 'Nay,
Custom as yours I can get any day.'

Then out of my pocket I took sovereigns bright,
And the landlady's eyes opened wide with delight,
She said, 'I have whiskies and wines of the best,
And the words that I said, sure, were only in jest.'

I'll go back to my parents, confess what I've done,
And ask them to pardon their prodigal son.
And if they caress me as they used to before,
Sure I never will play the wild rover no more.

Another song popular in Ireland with its audience appealing rhythmic clapping against the chorus, although its origin is uncertain.

43. The Black Velvet Band

Words and Music: Traditional

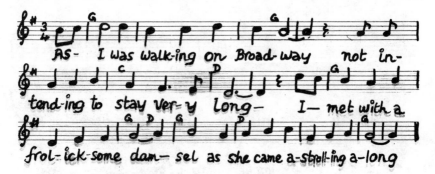

As I was walking on Broadway not intending to stay very long — I met with a frolicksome damsel as she came a-strolling along

Chorus:
And her eyes they were shining like diamonds
You'd think she was Queen of the land
And her hair hung over her shoulder
Tied up with a Black Velvet Band.

A watch she pulled out of her pocket
And placed it right into my hand
The very first day that I met her –
Bad luck to her Black Velvet Band. *Chorus:*

Before judge and jury next morning
Both of us had to appear
With a gentleman claiming his jewellery,
And the case up against us was clear. *Chorus:*

I got seven years transportation
Way down to Van Diemen's Land
Far away from my friends and companions
All account of the Black Velvet Band. *Chorus:*

A number which has crossed the Atlantic, received some American overtones and came back again, probably with changes in its original lyrics. Its energetic swing belies the rather tragic theme of transportation.

66

44. I'll Forgive Him

Words and Music: Traditional

When I was sing-le I wore a plaid shawl; now that I'm mar-ried I've noth-ing at all-oh, but still I love him I'll for-give him I'll go with him where-ev-er he goes

He comes down our alley and whistles me out
And when I get out there he knocks me about.

He stands at the corner and whistles me out
His hands in his pockets, his shirt hanging out.

He bought me a handkerchief red white and blue
Before I could use it he tore it in two.

We went to the alehouse; he bought me some stout
But before I could drink it he ordered me out.

There's cakes in the oven, and jam on the shelf
If you want anymore you can sing it yourself.

I suspect that this song would originally have been of English origin, but it became very much of the Irish scene in the ballad sessions of the mid and late 1960s. It was probably written in its original form over a hundred and fifty years ago.

45. Mrs Mulligan, The Pride of the Coombe

Words and Music: Dublic street ballad

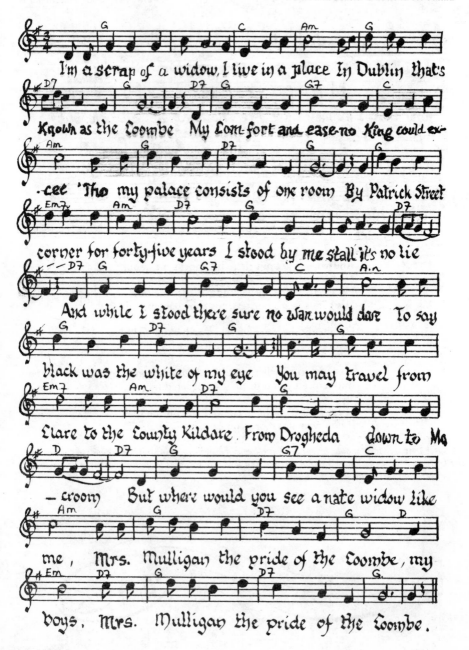

I'm a scrap of a widow, I live in a place In Dublin that's

known as the Coombe My comfort and ease no King could ex-

cee 'Tho my palace consists of one room By Patrick Street

corner for forty-five years I stood by me stall it's no lie

And while I stood there sure no wan would dare To say

black was the white of my eye You may travel from

Clare to the County Kildare. From Drogheda down to Ma

croon But where would you see a nate widow like

me, Mrs. Mulligan the pride of the Coombe, my

boys. Mrs. Mulligan the pride of the Coombe.

I sell apples and oranges, nuts and split peas,
  Bull's eyes and sugar stick sweet,
On a Saturday night I sell second-hand clothes
  From my stall on the floor of the street.
I have a son they call Micky, who plays on the fife,
  He is a member of the Longford Street Band,
It would do your heart good just to see them march out
  Of a Saturday to Sandymount Strand.

I sells fish every Friday laid out on a board
  The best you could catch in the sea
But the finest are herrings; sweet Dublin Bay herrings,
  That's best for your dinner and tea.
Every Sunday at Mass, shure I cuts quite a dash,
  All the neighbours look 'round in surprise
With me fine Paisley shawl, and me bonnet so tall,
  Shure I'd dazzle the sight of your eyes.

A Dublin street ballad, which was adapted in the 1920s and used as a 'theme song' by the inimitable Jimmy O'Dea in his character of Biddy Mulligan, the brash but loveable Dublin 'widow'.

69

BALLADS FROM THE PUBS OF IRELAND
James N. Healy

The well-loved songs in this book are the airs you heard sung in your favourite pub or whistled on the street, including 'The Jug of Punch', 'Whiskey in the Jar', 'The Shilling a Night', 'The Bould Tadhy Quill', 'Cockles and Mussels', 'The Croppy Boy', 'The Rising of the Moon' and 'The Moon Behind the Hill'.

LOVE SONGS OF THE IRISH
James N. Healy.

A collection of Ireland's best-loved traditional love songs ranging from the early seventeenth century to the present day — from Carolan to Thomas Moore to the contemporary John B. Keane.

BALLADS FROM AN IRISH FIRESIDE
James N. Healy

The well loved songs in this book are the airs you heard sung in your favourite pub or whistled on the street, including: 'Beautiful City', 'I Know My Love', 'The Ould Orange Flute', 'The Sive Song', 'Ronnie Reagan's Visit', 'Eileen Aroon', 'The Snowy Breasted Pearl', and 'The Dawning of the Day'.

THE SONGS OF PERCY FRENCH
James N. Healy

The well-loved songs in this volume are the airs you heard whistled on the street or sung in your favourite pub, including among others, 'The Mountains of Mourne', 'Phil the Fluther's Ball', 'Come Back Paddy Reilly', 'Are Ye Right There, Michael', 'The Darling Girl from Clare' and 'Shlatherty's Mounted Fut'. Percy French, Ireland's leading troubadour, was without doubt the most prolific of Irish song writers.